What *Love* Is

PHOTOGRAPHS BY LAURA STRAUS

Ariel Books

**Andrews McMeel
Publishing**

Kansas City

Photographs copyright © 2000 by Laura Straus, NY

ISBN: 0-7407-1083-4

Library of Congress Catalog Card Number: 00-100470

preface   I approached this project with great trepidation.

What is Love, after all? How could I possibly hope to find and capture it with my lens? Fortunately, Love revealed itself in a multitude of ways. There it was in the newfound feelings between Kristin and Matt, in their open faces and soft, playful hands. Love was at the wedding of Diana and Steve, who ran off to play together after the ceremony. It was there in the gaze of Abigail and Marco, dazzling and radiant as they made their vows in the summer twilight. And Love was found in the longer partnerships, too, in the mysterious and complicated relationship between Jack and Harriet leaning toward one another, and playing with my heart. Such fullness of spirit, at times passionate, at times wary, is what made the search for this ineffable, fragile, intangible quarry possible.

I am honored to have been able to learn from these friends, these lovers, these brave people who opened themselves to teach us what their Love is. I would like to thank Ariel Books, specifically Sue Carnahan and Armand Eisen, for making this book possible. My eternal gratitude to Jackie Decter and Judith Dupré for their encouragement and help, and most of all, thank you to each and every one of the participants, who taught me to look for the signs, because they are everywhere.

—Laura Straus

laughter

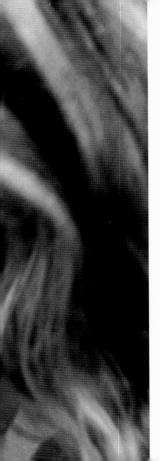

honest

comforting

pure joy!

commitment

existing for
each other

forever

a sensation

passionate

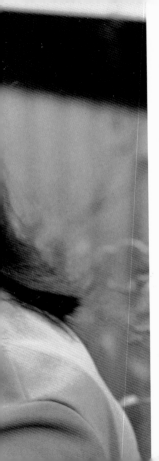

making up

building a
life together

sharing space

stolen moments

enjoying each other

intimate

finding each other

spontaneous

attending to
the details

never letting go

finding time

embracing

snuggling _____

being playful

Eskimo kisses!

celebrating

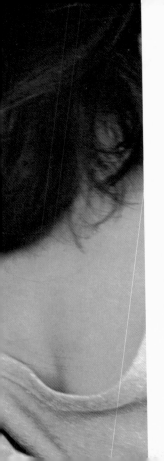

anticipation

looking toward
the future

vacationing

a walk in the park

timeless

This book was designed by BTDnyc

. . . AND TYPESET BY BTDNYC IN DUCHAMP BOLD AND SABON.